Y0-CXM-497

Table of Contents

Introduction

It is the purpose of this series of books to present students with information on important pathways across the Americas. The instructional activities have been carefully selected and organized to provide students with useful information as well as practice in developing needed skills. Since some students have difficulty learning with any degree of comprehension from the instructional materials they often encounter, a wide range of supplementary activities is provided. This is advantageous for all learners because the teacher can vary the instruction so each student is motivated to spend more time on task-related content activities.

The materials for guided practice were designed to maintain instructional momentum by expediting the business of learning through smooth transitions and creative choices. There are questions to answer, riddles to solve, charts to fill in, and content maps to create. Many of these require a little extra research in an atlas, almanac, encyclopedia, or road map. The history cards are meant for review purposes and also to inspire students to create more cards of their own to challenge classmates.

The lessons are designed for teachers who want students to be actively involved in their own learning. The material is not organized to conform to any conventional textbook; rather, it is organized to suit the purposes of the teacher who wants to either supplement or complement the textbook. The first page or two in each section provides student information. Student information pages are followed by activities that engage the student in both direct recall and application. Reproducible pages lead students to use higher-order thinking in a creative manner.

The informational pages can either be read to the students or duplicated for them to read by themselves or in small groups. The student activities can be done verbally by the teacher as a direct whole-class activity or used by students as independent activities. Many teachers may find it beneficial to place the simple diagrams and charts on the board or a transparency so students can copy the material directly into their notebooks. The action-oriented activities are designed to be done either individually as home projects or in groups with little direction from the teacher. This approach is beneficial for both teacher and student since students are given the responsibility for taking charge of their own learning and teachers can ensure that a variety of different learning styles is being addressed.

The purpose of this approach is to present implementation of instruction based on research-grounded procedures. The activities should 1) enhance recall of factual information, 2) improve comprehension of textual material, 3) provide opportunities for inquiry, and 4) involve students in both experiential and collaborative learning. As the student realizes the tie between the current activity and learning how to learn, the work will become more meaningful.

Ann Lockledge and Ted Henson

Soon after the Revolutionary War, American sailors visited ports in the Pacific Northwest to pick up furs. From there, they sailed to China to trade for tea and other exotic goods. But, once home, they told stories not only of the Far East, but of the beautiful forests on the other side of the continent.

Americans had first heard of the Oregon Country when Robert Gray and John Kendrick of Boston visited the area in 1788. By 1792, Gray had become the first American sea captain to sail into the Columbia River. At this time, the fur-trapping business was dominated by the British Hudson's Bay Company. The Russian fur traders were farther north.

In 1811, John Jacob Astor and his American Fur Company sent a ship to retrace Gray's route. They established Astoria, a trading post and fort at the mouth of the Columbia River. But during the War of 1812, Astor was forced to sell Astoria to the North West Company of Canada. Finally, in 1818, Britain and the United States agreed to jointly occupy the Oregon Country. It was decided that citizens of either country could use the Columbia River Valley.

A Boston schoolteacher named Hall Jackson Kelley was very interested in seeing that the Oregon region become totally American. He was able to convince a Massachusetts ice merchant, Nathaniel Wyeth, to create a company to develop the resources along the Columbia River. Wyeth managed to set up Fort Hall on the Snake River, but his business efforts were never successful. Nevertheless, the efforts of these two men kept people on the east coast aware of the Oregon Country.

One who helped establish good relations with the Indians was Dr. John McLoughlin of the Hudson's Bay Company. A Canadian fur trader who had been trained as a physician, he was sent in 1924 to be the company's agent and administrator in the Pacific Northwest. But his cooperative policies toward American settlers angered his superiors, and he retired in 1846.

In the meantime, the Americans had bought a land link to the Oregon Country. When Napoleon decided that he could not control the huge holding called Louisiana, he suddenly decided to sell it. The American Minister was a bold man who seized the opportunity and negotiated the purchase. While the Louisiana Purchase did not include Oregon, it provided the initiative for Americans to begin thinking of their country as going "from sea to shining sea."

Investigating the Oregon Country

REVIEWING THE READING

1. American sailors visited ports in the Pacific Northwest to buy _____ on their way to_____.

2. By 1792, Captain Robert Gray had become the first American sea captain to _____ _____.

3. A trading post at the mouth of the Columbia River called _____ was established by _____ _____ _____ in 1811.

4. Fort Hall was built by _____ _____ to develop the region and was named for Hall Jackson Kelley, a Boston _____.

5. Dr. John McLoughlin was a Hudson's Bay Company agent who established good relations with both _____ and _____ _____.

6. Finally, a land link to Oregon came with the_____ _____.

MAPPING THE MAJOR TERRITORIES

On the map below, color the different territories and write the names of at least three people, showing where they were influential.

When President Thomas Jefferson completed the Louisiana Purchase in April of 1803, the United States had suddenly grown by 800,000 square miles—double its former size. Since no one really knew much about this new territory, Congress set aside money to explore "the water communication across this continent." It was hoped that it would be possible to find a way to travel by water from the Mississippi River to the Pacific Ocean. The $2500 that was appropriated activated the secret plans that were already in place "to send intelligent officers with ten or twelve men, to explore even to the western ocean."

Two former army officers, one of whom was Jefferson's private secretary, were chosen to lead the expedition. The fact that going west of the Rockies would be moving into territory beyond the western boundary of the United States did not seem to bother either the president or Congress. And, due largely to the character and intelligence of its commanders, the expedition made a successful and safe crossing of thousands of miles of unknown territory. This gave the United States reason to claim the Oregon territory.

Meriwether Lewis and William Clark and a party of about 40 men set off on May 14, 1804. They planned to travel up the Missouri River as far as the Rocky Mountains before winter. In fact, they got only as far as the Mandan Indian country in what is now North Dakota. There, they engaged a French-Canadian fur trapper as a guide. It was his Shoshone wife, Sacajawea, who was the savior of the expedition. Carrying her small baby, she led the men through Indian country, persuading the Shoshone to help them on their way.

They planned to cover what they thought was a short distance from the mountains to the Columbia River, which had been discovered by Captain Gray eight years before. On reaching the Three Forks of the Missouri in July 1805, they chose to follow the most westerly of the three rivers. This took them through difficult country. Finally, after crossing the Continental Divide on August 12, they became convinced that the fabled water route did not exist. In September, the party reached the Clearwater River and traveled down it to the Snake and finally reached the Columbia. The discouraged party did not reach the Pacific Coast until November 1805.

A second winter was spent on the Pacific Coast, going over the information they had gathered. In March 1806, the expedition retraced its steps to the Continental Divide and then split into two groups. Clark led one party down the Yellowstone River, while Lewis's group descended the Missouri River. They rejoined in August on the Missouri and returned to Saint Louis in September. A huge area on the map of North America had now been explored. The American West, a place known only through rumor, had been opened to the American people.

Lewis and Clark Activities

REVIEWING THE READING

1. Who was president when the Louisiana Purchase was completed? _____
   _____

2. Who did he send to explore the "water communication" across the continent?
   _____and_____

3. How much money was set aside for the trip? _____

4. The savior of the expedition has more monuments to her than any other woman in
   American history. Who was she? _____

   Why do you think she is so popular? _____

5. Explain why you think rivers were used for travel and why you think Congress wanted
   them explored. _____
   _____

MAPPING THE EXPEDITION

On the map below: Color the Mississippi, Missouri, and Columbia rivers blue; mark the Rocky
Mountains in brown. Trace the route in green. Put a star (☆) on the capital of the United States.
Put a circle (○) where they spent the first winter and asterisks (*) where they spent the second.

The Mountain Men

In the early 1800s, a few hardy trappers followed Indian trails across the Rockies into Oregon. In their hunt for furs, some of the trappers made some useful discoveries. Jedediah Smith found South Pass in Wyoming, a plateau that offered an easy way to cross the Rocky Mountains. Manuel Lisa, a Spanish-American trapper, founded Fort Manuel, the first trading post on the upper Missouri. James Beckwourth, in his escape from slavery, discovered a pass through the Sierra Nevadas into California.

These mountain men dressed in shirts and trousers made of leather. Porcupine quills decorated their shirts. Around their necks they hung pouches carrying pipes, some tobacco, molds to make bullets, and other small things of value. During harsh winters, mountain men often lived with the Indians. They learned the language and the customs of their friends. From them they also learned the survival skills needed when living alone. Like the Indians, the trappers gorged themselves with food when game was plentiful. When meat was scarce, they lived off the land as well as they could.

During the fall and spring, the men tended their traps. But July was a time for getting together. They met fur traders at a place chosen the year before, called the rendezvous. At the rendezvous, everyone went wild. It was a time of singing, dancing, shouting, trading, running, jumping, racing, target-shooting, and storytelling. Since beaver hats were very popular with fashionable men in the East and Europe, they could bargain for a high price for their furs. Of course, the traders, in turn, charged high prices for the flour, bullets, and other supplies they hauled to the rendezvous.

The fur trade had drawn explorers to the West since early colonial times. The heyday of the mountain men began when William Henry Ashley and others went trapping on the upper Missouri River in 1822. It continued during the next 15 years, when trappers like James Bridger, Thomas Fitzpatrick, and Louis Vasquez explored the West. But by 1840, the fur trade had declined. The trappers had killed so many beavers that the animals were becoming scarce. Furthermore, beaver hats began going out of fashion. So the mountain men took on a new job of leading settlers along the rugged trail to Oregon.

Trappers and Traders

REVIEWING THE READING USING TWO WORDS

1. What name was used to refer to the fur-hunting trappers of the Rockies?

   _____ _____

2. What easy way to cross the Rocky Mountains was found by Jedediah Smith?

   _____ _____

3. Who built the first trading post on the upper Missouri?

   _____ _____

4. James Beckwourth found a pass through the _____ _____ coastal range.

5. The reason that furs brought a big price was the fashion of wearing _____ _____.

6. When the fur trade died, the men took on the job of _____ _____.

INVESTIGATING A LITTLE FARTHER

Choose one trapper from the reading and write a first-person account of that person's adventures. Tell where he went, what he saw, what he accomplished, and what you think he was feeling. Remember to look at things through the eyes of your mountain man. Use additional reference books to help collect more information.

Explorer Riddles

Unscramble the words to find the name of the explorer. Each was mentioned in your reading, but there may be more information here than you had before.

As one leader of an expedition to the Pacific coast, I was responsible for maintaining discipline and mapping the terrain. A few years later, I became Superintendent of Indian Affairs.

amwilil klrac _____

As private secretary to President Jefferson, I planned an expedition to find the Northwest Passage. I helped lead the first American group to the Pacific by an overland route. I was governor of the Louisiana Territory until I was shot and killed in 1809.

theemirewr welsi _____

I was one of the best-known mountain men. In order to escape slavery, I headed west from Virginia and discovered a pass through the Sierra Nevadas into California. In 1856, I added to my own fame by having my life story published.

samje cworbuketh _____

I found the South Pass in Wyoming in 1823. This broad plateau offered an easy way for the Oregon Trail to cross the Rocky Mountains. You may have seen a movie about me.

deeidjah himts _____

I was a Spanish-American trapper who led a trip up the Missouri River in 1807. I founded a Fort that was named for me and became the first outpost on the upper Missouri.

leumna sail _____

I was an American fur trapper, guide, and Indian agent who escorted missionary parties to the Northwest. In 1841, I guided the first wagon train of settlers to California. I also accompanied Fremont's 1843-44 expedition.

somtha tritfazpkic _____

The pioneering Jesuit missionary Pierre Jean De Smet from Belgium had great influence among the Indians of North America. After founding a mission in Iowa, he established a mission near the present-day site of Missoula, Montana. The most important missions that he opened in the Northwest were along the Willamette River in Oregon. Because of his courage and winning personality, De Smet earned the respect of Northwestern and Plains tribes and was welcome to travel among them.

A group of Protestant missionaries opened new stretches of the Oregon Trail in 1836. Reports from these travelers and from Father De Smet encouraged others to make the trip to Oregon to establish farms. The resulting flood of settlers began in the spring of 1843, when about 1,000 men, women, and children gathered at Independence with their wagons to make the six-month trek. By 1846 more than 6,000 people had used the trail.

However, the discovery of gold in California in 1848 reduced the flow of traffic to Oregon, and by the 1860s the flood on the trail had dwindled to a trickle. However, the resentment of the Native Americans of the flow of people into land they considered their own continued to grow.

A medical doctor and pioneer Presbyterian missionary, Marcus Whitman, established the most famous mission in Oregon Country. After first going west in 1835 to select mission sites, he returned in 1836 with his new wife, Narcissa, and a small brave group of missionaries. Narcissa Whitman, one of the first white women in the region, had the courage and determination to match that of her husband. Together they founded a mission among the Cayuse Indians west of present Walla Walla, Washington. It did not fare well, however, and, in 1843, Whitman returned east to persuade the board not to abandon the project.

On his journey back Whitman helped guide the first large party of settlers to Oregon. After this, his mission became an important stopping place for westward-bound settlers. Unfortunately, these travelers also brought with them diseases that caused many deaths among the Indian tribes. The Indians blamed the Whitmans for a measles outbreak among their people. After a period of growing hostility, a band of Cayuse massacred Whitman, his family, and several others in 1847.

Thinking About the Missionaries

REVIEWING THE READING

1. Who was the Catholic missionary who was able to get along with the Indians? _____
   _____

2. Where did he establish missions?_____ _____ _____

3. Who was the Protestant missionary who was blamed for bringing disease to the Indian tribes? _____

4. Where was his mission? _____

5. What was the disease for which the Indians had no immunity? _____

6. What happened to Narcissa Whitman?_____
   _____

DISCUSSION GUIDE

1. Why do you think these missionaries were willing to brave the hardships of life in Oregon Country? _____
   _____
   _____
   _____
   _____

2. Why do you think the Indian tribes reacted differently to different missionaries?_____
   _____
   _____
   _____
   _____

3. There were many "seeds of change" that resulted from the coming of Europeans to this continent. Some were good—some bad. Why do you think disease might be numbered among them? _____
   _____
   _____
   _____
   _____

Oregon Trail People History Cards

On the following pages is material about people who were important to the history of the Oregon Trail. Cut out each rectangle and glue it onto a 5" x 8" card. Punch holes after each possible answer. On the back, circle the hole of the correct answer.

SAMPLE

The Trail

Americans began traveling west from Independence, Mo. They were headed to Oregon.

The Oregon Trail started in:
Independence •
St. Louis •
Omaha •

Front of Card

⊙
•
•

Back of Card

Sacajawea

Sacajawea was a Shoshone Indian woman who married a French trapper and guide, Toussaint Charbonneau. With Sacajawea carrying her small baby, they accompanied Lewis and Clark to the Pacific Northwest. She was invaluable as an interpreter and in making arrangements with the Shoshone people, whose country lay along the expedition's route. She and her husband later settled for a time on a farm near St. Louis. Some say she died of a fever at Fort Manuel in South Dakota in 1812; others claim that she lived until 1884 at the Shoshone Agency in Wyoming.

To what Indian tribe did Sacajawea belong?

a. Shoshone
b. Sioux
c. Mandan

Who was she able to help?

a. Charbonneau
b. South Dakotans
c. Lewis and Clark

Meriwether Lewis

Meriwether Lewis was co-commander of the first government-sponsored expedition that went all the way to the Pacific by an overland route. A former army officer, he was private secretary to President Thomas Jefferson from 1801 to 1803. By the conclusion of the Louisiana purchase, he had already made plans for the expedition. Soon after his triumphant return, he was appointed governor of the Louisiana Territory. Not long after, while traveling to Washington on official business, he was shot and killed. Even today, the reason for the killing remains a mystery.

What was Lewis' job before he led the expedition?

a. accountant
b. officer in the navy
c. private secretary

What was Lewis' job after he returned from Oregon?

a. officer
b. governor of Louisiana
c. commander

William Clark

William Clark, the brother of George Rogers Clark, was one of the captains of the Lewis and Clark expedition. He took on the responsibility for mapping the land they traveled. He also was in charge of maintaining military discipline. After their return, he arranged publication of the records of the journey. In 1807 he was appointed superintendent of Indian affairs and helped shape the federal government's policy in the West. Among the Indian tribes, he was known as "red-haired chief." Clark was also governor of the Missouri Territory for several years.

What was Clark's main job during the trip?

a. arranging publications
b. Superintendent of Indians
c. mapping the terrain

What was a position he held after the expedition returned?

a. governor of Missouri Territory
b. Indian chief
c. Chief of Publications

Manuel Lisa

Manuel Lisa was a Spanish-American fur trapper who led an expedition to the upper Missouri River in 1809. He was one of the first of the mountain men who opened the West for the pioneers who were to come. He established the first fur-trading post on the Big Horn River, but it was eventually destroyed by hostile Indians. He also founded Fort Manuel, an important landmark along the Oregon Trail.

What fort along the Oregon Trail was named for this fur trapper?

a. Fort Lisa
b. Fort Manuel
c. Fort Big Horn

Fur trappers helped open the West.

a. true
b. false

Marcus Whitman

Marcus Whitman was a medical doctor and Presbyterian missionary who, along with his wife Narcissa, founded a mission among the Cayuse Indians. After Whitman returned east to persuade the mission board not to abandon the project, he helped guide the first large party of settlers to Oregon. Afterwards, his mission became an important stopping place for pioneers on the Oregon Trail. Unfortunately, these travelers brought with them diseases such as measles that caused many Indians to die. Eventually, the Cayuse massacred the Whitmans and 12 others who were at the mission.

Whitman founded a mission among what Indian tribe?

a. Sioux
b. Cayuse
c. Presbyterian

The Cayuse were angry with the Whitmans because:

a. They were missionaries.
b. Mrs. Whitman nursed white babies.
c. Travelers brought bad diseases.

Father Pierre Jean De Smet

After arriving in the United States from Belgium in 1821, Pierre Jean De Smet became a Catholic missionary among the Indians of North America. His courage and powerful personality earned him the respect of the people he came to serve. First, he founded a mission among the Potawatomi Indians at Council Bluffs, Iowa, and then established Saint Mary's mission near present-day Missoula, Montana. This was Montana's first permanent white settlement. By 1844 he had opened the most important mission in the Northwest on the Willamette River in Oregon. Although asked by the church to stop active missionary work, he was able to continue traveling among the tribes as a peacemaker for many years.

Father De Smet was:

a. a missionary to Belgium
b. respected by the Indians
c. an emigrant from Council Bluffs

The first permanent mission in Montana was founded:

a. on the Willamette River
b. at Council Bluffs
c. before 1844

Jedediah Smith

Jedediah Strong Smith was a leader among the mountain men and fur trappers of the west. He traveled extensively throughout the region and in 1824 discovered the South Pass, a gateway to the Far West. This broad plateau offered an easy way for the Oregon Trail to cross the Rocky Mountains. It was Smith's journeys that opened the overland routes to California through the Sierra Nevadas and the overland trail from California to the Columbia River. He was killed leading a covered-wagon train along the Santa Fe Trail.

What was Smith's most important contribution to the Oregon Trail?

a. a way past the Sierra Nevadas
b. a route from the overland trail
c. South Pass in the Rockies

Jedediah Smith traveled most of the important trails of the West.

a. true
b. false

James Beckwourth

James Beckwourth was one of the best-known mountain men. The son of a Virginia slave, he headed west to escape slavery. He discovered a pass, through the Sierra Nevadas into California, that was named for him. In 1856, Beckwourth added to his own legend by publishing his life story. The founding of Pueblo, Colorado, is credited to Beckwourth, who arrived with his party in 1842 to set up a trading post for Rocky Mountain fur traders and trappers.

James Beckwourth was:

a. Anglo
b. African-American
c. Spanish-American

Beckwourth founded the city of:

a. Pueblo, Colorado
b. Sierra Nevada, California
c. Willamette, Oregon

Pioneers on the Oregon Trail met up with a great many different Indian tribes. Many of them are identified today by the language they spoke in common rather than customs they followed.

The Cheyenne were famous as horse-riding hunter-warriors on the Great Plains. These Algonquian-speakers originally lived as farmers in Minnesota until they began migrating westward. When Lewis and Clark met them, they were living as nomadic buffalo hunters in the Black Hills of South Dakota. They later settled along the Cheyenne River of North Dakota.

The Sioux was one of the most influential of the Indian nations of the Great Plains because it represented such a powerful example of Indian thought and life. The Sioux language is spoken in various dialects by tribes across the United States. The main Sioux groups include the Lakota, Dakota, Oglala Sioux, and Blackfoot. Together, the Sioux numbered about 30,000 people by 1850. They were outstanding warriors, fighting not only hostile tribes but also white intruders and the army troops that protected them.

The Crow call themselves the Absoraka, which in their Sioux language means "bird people." They left their villages along the Missouri River and moved westward toward the Rocky Mountains. The tribe became famous as hunters and warriors and later as scouts for the U.S. Army. Like other Plains people, the Crow depended on the buffalo for food and skins and on the horse for transportation. They lived in portable tipis and used rawhide for containers, moccasins, and shields.

Chinook-speaking groups were numerous and prosperous. Indians from the distant interior congregated at The Dalles on the Lower Columbia to trade furs, mountain-sheep horns, and war captives for salmon, coastal shells, and other goods exchanged by the Chinook. The simple Chinook communications system was adopted and spread by white traders of the eighteenth century. The incursion of the North West Company and Hudson's Bay Company into the Columbia River region in the early nineteenth century broke the Chinook trade monopoly and introduced European diseases that decimated the Indians. From an estimated population of about 16,000 in 1805, their numbers were reduced to only about 100 by the 1850s.

The great Sioux chiefs such as Red Cloud, Sitting Bull, Crazy Horse, and Black Elk were dedicated to keeping alive their unique life, religion, and culture. It was a culture characterized by outstanding horsemanship, an economy based on the buffalo, vision quests, soldier societies, and sacred dances. These chiefs were articulate in their objections to the white man and his ways. They believed in the self-discipline that had developed because of the hardships of their nomadic life. From this had come a sense of community and an instinctive desire to live with nature.

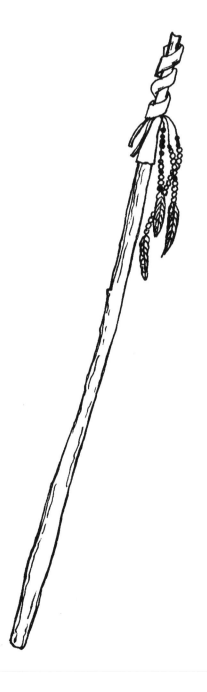

The Sioux had an elaborate and sophisticated code of moral, religious, and social behavior. To them, fighting was based on valor and bravery, so they might simply touch an enemy to represent a kill and then let him live. It was the truthful recital of the event that brought a man honor and prestige. The chiefs were not savages blindly resisting white civilization because they did not understand it. They were political, military, and spiritual leaders who found the white culture inferior to their own. Even when they lost, it did not shake their conviction that their ways were superior to those of their conquerors.

When leaders were faced with making an important decision that would affect their people, they discussed the matter by allowing everyone to have a chance to have their say. An object, often a decorated stick, was passed around to designate the speaker. Whoever was holding the talking stick was the only one to speak and no one was allowed to interrupt him.

You can make a talking stick to use during group discussions. Use a stick that has been cleaned of leaves and bark. String some beads on fish line and tape or tie feathers to the end. Wind yarn, ribbons, or rawhide around the stick. Add your beaded string.

Talking Stick Discussions

In small groups, you are going to use a talking stick to help guide the discussion. Remember 1) everyone must have a chance to have their say and 2) whoever is holding the talking stick is the only one allowed to speak and no one is allowed to interrupt. Take time to do a little research and to make notes before you begin to speak.

CONSIDER: The Cheyenne were an Algonquian-speaking Indian people who lived as nomadic buffalo hunters. They became famous throughout the Great Plains for their skill at fighting on horseback. Often at war with other tribes such as the Kiowa and Comanche, they formed alliances to fight white settlers and the U.S. Army. At the infamous Sand Creek Massacre, from 150 to 500 Cheyenne were killed. This led to their playing an important role in the defeat of General George Custer at the Battle of the Little Big Horn in 1876.

DECIDE: If the Spanish had not brought horses to the New World, how might the life of the Cheyenne have been different?

_____

_____

_____

DECIDE: If the Cheyenne had been Sioux-speaking instead of Algonquian-speaking, might they have done less fighting?

_____

_____

_____

DECIDE: Since the Kiowa and the Comanche were often at war with the Cheyenne, why do you think they were willing to join in alliances in fighting the white man?

_____

_____

_____

DECIDE: If Colonel Chivington had not killed so many Cheyenne at Sand Creek, might General Custer not have had to make his last stand?

_____

_____

_____

Native-American History Cards

Here are more history cards for you to make. Cut out each rectangle and glue it onto a 5" x 8" card. Punch holes after each possible answer. On the back, circle the hole of the correct answer.

Washakie

Washakie, a Shoshone chief in Wyoming, will be remembered for his friendship with the white pioneers. He was famous as a warrior when his tribe was fighting the Blackfoot and the Crow. Then, from time to time, he served as a scout for the U.S. Army during its campaigns against the Sioux and Cheyenne. When wagon trains were passing through Shoshone country in the 1850s, Washakie and his people helped the Oregon-bound travelers ford streams and round up stray cattle.

Washakie was a friend of the:
a. white man
b. Blackfoot
c. Cheyenne

Washakie was always a peaceful man.
a. true
b. false

Sitting Bull

Sitting Bull, a chief of the Hunkpapa Lakota, led his people against those who came into Sioux territory. He was known for having the virtues most admired by the Sioux: bravery, fortitude, generosity, and wisdom. After the successful attack on Custer at the Little Bighorn in 1876, Sitting Bull and other Sioux fled to Canada. When he returned in 1881, he was imprisoned for two years before being allowed to return to Standing Rock. Some people feel that the reason he was allowed to travel with Buffalo Bill and his Wild West Show was to keep him away from the reservation.

Sitting Bull was known for:
a. fleeing to Canada
b. fighting with Buffalo Bill
c. attacking General Custer

The Sioux admired bravery, fortitude, generosity, and wisdom.
a. true
b. false

Red Cloud

Red Cloud, a chief of the Oglala Sioux, fought every attempt of the whites to take territory that he felt belonged to his people. For years he was able to keep the United States government from opening the West. In 1860 he and his band came onto Indian territory along the North Platte River. Later, after signing a peace treaty, he agreed to settle down as a reservation chief. Sitting Bull and Crazy Horse, among others, felt that he sold out to the whites.

Red Cloud was known for:
a. attacking people coming into Indian territory
b. selling out to the whites
c. being a friend of Crazy Horse

One reason the army had trouble opening up the West was:
a. a lack of good roads
b. the North Platte River
c. attacks on white immigrants

During the 1830s traders and explorers began to tell stories about an area called the Oregon Country. The farmland was said to be fertile, the streams plentiful with fish, and the weather mild. Dreaming the dream, thousands of pioneers traveled to Missouri to join wagon trains headed west. They set out on a six-month trip along the Oregon Trail.

Americans also heard about riches south of the Oregon Country in California. They traveled the Oregon Trail and then broke off along the California Trail. When gold was discovered in California, 80,000 49ers raced to California. Few found gold but many stayed because of the rich farmlands and mild weather.

During the 1840s and 1850s, the Oregon Trail stretched about 2,000 miles from Independence, Missouri, to Fort Vancouver. It carried thousands of American pioneers to the rich farmland of the Willamette Valley in the Oregon Country. The main trail ran west and then northwest to Fort Kearny (in present Nebraska), then west again along the Platte and North Platte rivers to Fort Laramie. It went through the Rockies via South Pass, turned north to Fort Hall, followed the Snake River to Fort Boise, and then moved northwest to the Columbia River. The trail's last stretch was the Columbia itself, usually navigated by raft to Fort Vancouver.

Explorers, fur trappers, and traders opened parts of the route during the first third of the nineteenth century. Reports from missionary families and from Father Pierre De Smet encouraged others to make the trip to Oregon to establish farms. The resulting "Oregon fever" broke out in the spring of 1843, when about 1,000 men, women, and children gathered at Independence with their wagons to make the six-month trek. By 1846, more than 6,000 people had used the trail. The discovery of gold in California in 1848 reduced the flow of traffic to Oregon, and, by the 1860s, use of the trail had dwindled considerably.

The pioneers organized themselves into small companies, and strict discipline was required because of the perilous nature of the route. Indian attacks, cholera epidemics, grass fires, storms, and floods were among the many hazards. The trail passed through stretches of barren country, and people and animals alike frequently faced fatigue and hunger.

On to Oregon

REVIEWING THE READING

1. Traders and explorers began to tell stories of an area called _____ _____ in the 1830s.

2. In the 1840s and 1850s, the Oregon Trail stretched from _____ to Fort Vancouver.

3. The discovery of _____ in California reduced the number of people going to Oregon.

4. The trip over the Oregon Trail lasted about _____ months.

5. The rush for Oregon resulting in "Oregon Fever" started in the spring of _____.

COMPUTE AN ANSWER

The journey over the Oregon Trail usually took about six months. The distance covered was 2,000 miles. Calculate the average distance a settler was able to travel in one day on the trail. (Hint: Use 30 as the average number of days in a month.)

_____

MAKING A DECISION

Imagine that you and your family have decided to move to Oregon in 1843. You have been asked to make a list of items you will take with you that your family will need for the 2,000-mile journey. Remember that you will be traveling with a horse-drawn wagon. Make your list below and give a reason for taking each item. Continue your list on another sheet of paper. Be specific in your list. For example, don't just write "food"; tell what kind of food you might take.

Items to be taken	Reason for taking
_____	_____
_____	_____
_____	_____
_____	_____
_____	_____
_____	_____

Great Trails of the West

On the U.S. map below, mark and label the Oregon Trail with a dark black or red line. Also mark and label trails that led off from the Oregon Trail, such as the Santa Fe Trail, the Mormon Trail, and the California Trail, with dotted lines. Label places along the trails and write some of the things that might have been happening in each particular spot.

Life on the Oregon Trail was a mixture of hardship, danger, and adventure. The trip, which took about six months, was often begun with a covered wagon. But many of the pioneers walked, pushing handcarts loaded with a few precious possessions. The heavy and awkward Conestoga wagons covered with sailcloth and pulled by oxen were fine in the prairies but did not do well in the mountains. It became dangerous to ford streams and cross mountains. To lighten the wagons, travelers threw away gear. Soon the trails were marked by blacksmiths' anvils, plows, large grindstones, baking ovens, kegs, barrels, harnesses, and clothing. It was there for the taking for anyone who could bring it along.

The trail was never easy. Rivers had to be crossed, even when they were flooded. Travelers could become ill from cholera and other diseases. Babies became sick from the heat or the altitude. But the wagon train would not wait for them to feel better. Wagon axles broke and coyotes howled at night. Even though families had packed enough dried food, such as beans or corn, to last throughout the journey, fresh meat and wood were sometimes hard to find. The settlers often found only unsafe water holes when they needed fresh water for themselves and their animals. They used leather bags to hold water for the dry stretches between rivers.

Once the wagon train was formed, its members elected a captain to lead them. Men familiar with the trail were hired as guides. The wagons without livestock led the way. At the end of the day, they stopped to make camp. A few hours later, the slower part of the wagon train would reach the camp and draw into the circle. This circle provided added protection in case of Indian attacks and kept the cattle from wandering off to find grass. Within the protective ring, the travelers found the companionship that helped fight the loneliness of traveling mile after mile without seeming to get anywhere.

Families adapted quickly to life on the trail. At dawn, everyone woke to a bugle blast or the ringing of a bell or striking of a large triangle. Each person had a job to do. Young girls helped their mothers prepare breakfast. Men and boys harnessed the horses or oxen. By six o'clock, the cry of "Wagons ho!" could be heard as the first of the column again began the long trek across the plains.

Living the Life of the Trail

REVIEWING THE READING

1. Many pioneers traveled the 2,000-mile Oregon Trail in a wagon, but others walked pushing a _____.

2. A _____ wagon was covered with sailcloth and pulled by oxen.

3. The wagon trains formed a protective circle at night to _____ and to _____.

4. Leather bags were used to carry _____ for dry stretches between the _____.

5. A _____ was elected to lead each wagon train, and men familiar with the trail were hired as _____.

HARDSHIPS FACED BY TRAVELERS ON THE OREGON TRAIL

Imagine that you are traveling on the Oregon Trail. Make a list of the hardships that you have to face as you travel along the trail. Make your list below and then compare it with another person's list to see if you missed anything.

_____

_____

_____

_____

_____

_____

On a separate piece of paper, write a diary entry from one day of your travels. Be certain that you write about the good times as well as the hardships you might have faced. Identify the day and tell where you are.

Mountain man Jim Bridger had warned all of the people at Fort Kearny to be on the lookout for Indians crawling along under wolf robes. He knew that they would hide among the real wolves drawn by the slaughter house outside the fort walls. Bridger would point to the flash of tin mirrors but the sparkle was ignored. "It's only sunlight striking on the edge of sharp stone!" he was informed. He had warned that real wolf howls had no echo, but the imitated howls of spies did. And spies from Chief Red Cloud came all the time on faked errands so they would know what was going on at the fort.

One winter day, Captain Fetterman and 80 men went out from the fort to help protect a mule train that was hauling firewood from a pine woods seven miles away. He and his men were not really ready. The soldiers were clumsy riders compared to the Indians, who rode their ponies bareback, zigging and zagging as they fired their guns or shot their arrows. The soldiers had been trained to dismount and take slow, sure aim. Spies inside the fort signaled to Oglala Chief Red Cloud with their mirrors. He knew the troopers were coming and he knew they were not taking the danger seriously.

Indians rushed the troopers and then pretended to retreat. Fetterman rushed after them into an ambush. As he disappeared over a ridge, the fort heard a great deal of rapid firing and then— nothing. A Lieutenant Ten Eyck with 54 men hurried in the direction of the sounds of battle but they found only dead bodies. Not only had the Sioux killed every soldier, but they had disappeared with the guns and bullets.

Unfortunately for the Sioux, they thought that they would be able to repeat their victory the following year. The man in charge this time listened to the warnings. He formed a circle fort by turning on their sides the heavy wagon-boxes that were used to haul the wood. He was also prepared with extra rifles behind each sharpshooter. This time the men did not have to use rifles that were too hot to the touch from having been fired repeatedly. Fire arrows had no effect because the major had chosen a hill with little or no dry grass. Red Cloud had to retreat from the second charge. He had lost 1,137 warriors to the soldiers' three.

Fighting the Fight

REVIEWING THE READING

1. _____ was the mountain man who tried to warn the people at Fort Kearny to be on the lookout for Indians.

2. Spies of Chief _____ came to the fort on fake errands to see what was happening.

3. Captain _____ led 80 men out of the fort to protect a mule team that was hauling _____ from a pine woods.

4. The Indians were able to ambush the troops, killing everyone and taking the _____ and _____.

5. A year later, _____ had to retreat from a second charge against troops from the fort and lost _____ warriors to the soldiers' three.

THINKING IT OVER

1. Discuss the Fetterman Massacre with a partner. List as many reasons as you can why the Indians under Red Cloud were able to defeat Fetterman's troops.

   _____

   _____

   _____

2. What were the reasons that the second attempted ambush by Red Cloud was unsuccessful? What changes had been made by the troops at Fort Kearny? List as many as possible below.

   _____

   _____

   _____

   _____

3. What lessons should the troops and their commanders at Fort Kearny have learned from this experience against Red Cloud? What advice would you have given if you had been asked to make recommendations for the protection of troops at the fort?

   _____

   _____

   _____

   _____

Cultural Differences

In the boxes below, illustrate the cultural differences between Native Americans and settlers on the Oregon Trail.

A. Indians never felt that they owned a piece of land. Individual ownership was nothing they understood. The tribe would claim a certain area for a brief period of time and then move on. When settlers came, they had stakes to mark the boundaries of homesteads. This non-Indian built fences to keep in his cattle and horses, to claim that it was his land. Indians did not understand how an individual could think he owned land, because it had existed long before that person was born.

SETTLER	NATIVE AMERICAN

B. The new settlers had ties to Europe, where kings ruled and titles were passed from father to eldest son. Indians chose a chief because his deeds and his character qualified him for such leadership. The newcomers thought of a chief as a king and did not understand that a chief's son did not inherit his father's leadership role. A chief's son, just like any other young man of the tribe, proved his manhood to his tribe and to himself by his own deeds.

SETTLER	NATIVE AMERICAN

C. The Indians had many ways to send messages, such as smoke signals, sign language, and pictographs, which the settlers did not understand. They thought Indians should learn their languages but not the other way around. Since they had little understanding of the Indian language, they failed to translate ideas properly. An Indian could not respect anyone who talked too fast or too much. It was not his way. Indians never answered questions right away. They believed in stopping to think before speaking to show respect to the questioner. The newcomers thought this discourteous.

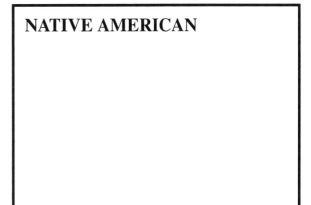

D. Indians thought the newcomers foolish for covering themselves from head to foot with tight and clumsy clothes. To them, fresh air and sunshine nourished the body just like food. The settler, on the other hand, considered the Indian uncivilized for wearing no more than a breechcloth. He considered the hair on his own face, chest, arms, and legs manly. But this disgusted the Indian, who believed that the head was the only place hair should be allowed to grow long.

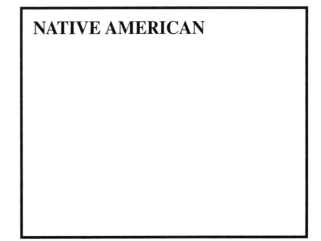

One of the great heroes of the railroad-building era of the overland trail was General Grenville Dodge. General Dodge had fought the Indians and later had them working for him during the Civil War. He knew his enemy and never underestimated them. Generals Dodge and Custer once met after a good dinner provided by the railroad's eastern office. Custer was boasting that a well-trained white soldier with a decent horse could defeat any six Indians. Dodge replied, "Custer, that may be brave but it is no longer true. It is rash madness. You talk like a fool. The Indian has learned a lot in a century." Later, Custer found that Dodge knew what he was talking about.

Dodge was the construction engineer of the Union Pacific railroad. He began to realize that he was not going to be able to lay his rails alongside the rippling waters of the Sweetwater River. No matter how dangerous, he had to go through the mountains. He was meeting with officials from Washington in Laramie when a rider on an exhausted horse came dashing up to the post. He reported that Percy Brown's engineering party had been terribly beaten by 300 Sioux. From dawn to nightfall, Brown and 13 men had been under attack on an elevation in the Great Basin. Although he asked his men to leave him there, they made a litter of their cabins and carried Brown 12 miles to a stage station. He died within an hour.

One of the government commissioners suggested that Dodge halt all work for six months until there was more military support. Dodge refused. As he wrote to a financial backer, "If we stop now we may never get started again." He knew that Congressional enemies of the railroads would dump the whole project. The railroad would not get the land grant with which they could issue bonds to keep the cash coming. "I'll push this road on to Salt Lake in another year or surrender my own scalp to the Indians," he wrote to a friend.

When he reached the North Platte, he found that it was at flood stage because of the snow that was melting high in the mountains. Two young officers tried to get across but were swept back to their starting point. The rest of the company would not even try. Dodge jumped on his horse, Rocky Mountain, and plunged into the water. "If you are going to help me build the Union Pacific, you have to learn to swim horses across more rivers than this one," he shouted to the men. They all made it across by helping one another.

Railroads and the West

REVIEWING THE READING

1. General _____ was a construction engineer for the Union Pacific Railroad.

2. General Dodge gained his knowledge of Indians by _____ them and then having them work for him during the _____.

3. Dodge was meeting with officials from _____ when he heard about the defeat of _____ engineering party by the Sioux.

4. One _____ suggested that Dodge stop work for six months until there was more _____ support.

5. Dodge found the _____ at flood stage because of the _____ melting high in the mountains.

THINKING IT OVER

1. Give as many reasons as possible for Grenville Dodge to be called one of the great heroes of the railroad-building era of the overland trail.

   _____

   _____

   _____

2. General Dodge rode across the flooded North Platte River on his horse, Rocky Mountain. How did this action show courage?

   _____

   _____

   _____

3. Why do you think that his men were then able to cross the river after this act?

   _____

   _____

   _____

4. What leadership skills did General Dodge demonstrate at the North Platte?

   _____

   _____

   _____

Jim Bridger knew the wagons were coming—coming in hordes. He figured that he could do a big business selling supplies and repairing wagons if he would just establish a stopping place. Around 1838, he built himself a fort west of South Pass on the Green River where the snow was not so deep. Spring came earlier there, the water was pure, the trout plentiful, and the buffalo available.

Bridger had found South Pass when he was coming from the west. Some hostile Indian raiding parties made going back the way they had come very dangerous. He worked his way south and came through what came to be known as South Pass to the Platte River. This passage became the preferred route for the Missouri fur traders who were coming upriver to purchase the valuable beaver pelts.

The outer wall of the new Fort Bridger was built of pickets which were stuck in the ground and covered with adobe mud. The adobe dried rock-hard in the sun. The gate was made of strong timber, thick enough to be arrow- and bullet-proof. Inside the walls were two or three 40-foot-long cabins with adobe floors. Because the roofs were adobe, they were not only fire-resistant but also provided insulation against heat and cold. Bridger even discovered coal near his fort, which could be used in the cabin fireplaces.

Goats, milk cows, and ponies were kept inside the walls. Here, also, were the supplies that were brought in with great effort from the east. And, most importantly, this is where the furs brought by trappers were stored.

While Bridger traveled hither and yon as hunter, trader, and guide, he left his partner to keep the books and do the trading. He and Louis Vasquez were presently reaping a fortune. Rich tourists/hunters were not always impressed by Fort Bridger. Overland travelers saw it as a marvelous source of supplies, help, and safety. They did not mind the 25 to 50 Indian tipis that were always to be seen outside the walls.

Bridger did not keep his children at the fort. He sent his little daughter to Walla Walla to be educated by the Whitmans. He knew Dr. Whitman from when he cut a Blackfoot arrowhead from the mountain man's shoulder at the rendezvous of 1835. After the massacre at the Whitmans', he sent his other children with Father De Smet to be educated in the Indian schools run by the Catholic church in St. Louis.

A Western Fort

REVIEWING THE READING

1. Jim Bridger planned to do a big business selling _____ and repairing _____ for settlers headed west.

2. Fort Bridger was built west of _____ on the _____ River.

3. In what two ways did the adobe roofs offer protection for the cabins of the fort?

   _____

   _____

4. Bridger sent his daughter to _____ to be educated by the _____.

5. His other children were sent with _____ to be educated in the Indian schools run by the Catholic church in _____.

COMPARING WHAT PEOPLE REMEMBER

Different people who were at the same place at the same time might have very different memories of the same events. That would likely be true of people who saw the westward movement along the Oregon Trail. In the chart below, tell what you think each person would remember 20 years afterwards.

MEMORIES FROM DIFFERENT PERSPECTIVES

Memories	Mountain Man	Sioux Warrior	Pioneer
How I traveled:			
Problems I faced:			
What I saw:			
How I used the land:			
People I knew:			
Things I did for fun:			

Choose one of these people and interview him or her as if you were a newspaper reporter. Write what you think would be the results.

From Independence to Omaha

Across the Missouri River and into what is now the state of Kansas, past Fort Leavenworth, and on to Omaha was the first leg of the Oregon Trail.

The first permanent settlement at the junction of the Kansas and Missouri Rivers was a trading post established in 1821. Several small villages were founded nearby in the years that followed. Among these was Independence, the starting point of the Oregon Trail. The towns prospered as they were the beginning point for westward expeditions. This prosperity, however, was interrupted from time to time by epidemics of various diseases. Economic stability was finally ensured by the arrival of railroad lines in 1865. The name Kansas City became official for the area on both sides of the river in the late 1880s.

Just north of Kansas City is St. Joseph, which was founded in 1843 by Joseph Robidoux, a French-Canadian trapper. This city, too, flourished as a ferry point on the Missouri River and a base for pioneers. In 1860, it became the starting point of the Pony Express.

On the trail is the city of Leavenworth, which is south of the Old Fort Leavenworth which guarded settlers along the trail. The fort was established in 1827 by Col. Henry Leavenworth and hosted travelers on both the Santa Fe and Oregon Trails in the 1830s and 1840s. The present-day city was begun illegally in 1854, when a group of pro-slavery Missourians set up a town site on land belonging to the Delaware Indians. In 1857 it became the headquarters of the Pony Express, which sped the mail on to Sacramento, California, in as little as nine days.

Omaha is a city in eastern Nebraska on the Missouri River opposite Council Bluffs, Iowa. The site was occupied by the Omaha Indians until a treaty opened the Nebraska Territory to settlement in 1854. The city was the territorial capital from 1855 to 1867, and it grew as an outfitting point for westward-bound settlers, with steamboats arriving regularly. In 1865 the Union Pacific, the first transcontinental railroad, began moving westward from Omaha. The railroad built stockyards there in the 1880s, and the great meat-packing houses followed. Council Bluffs was settled by Mormons in 1846 and called Kanesville until 1852. The new name was given in honor of the council with local Indians held in 1804 by Meriwether Lewis and William Clark.

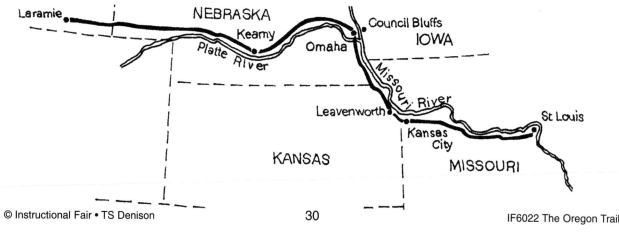

The main trail ran west from Omaha and then northwest to Fort Kearny and then west again along the Platte and North Platte Rivers to Fort Laramie. The direction of all overlanders was up the Platte along the north bank, the south bank, or by shortcut across the Big Blue and Little Blue Rivers.

Just like Fort Leavenworth, Fort Kearny was established to act as a check on the tribes of marauding Indians. It was the first army post on this part of the trail. Built to protect the trail, it became a haven for tired travelers, a welcome stagecoach stop, and a needed pony express relay station.

Fort Kearny saw two of the most terrible battles in all frontier history—the Fetterman Massacre and the Wagon-Box Fight. In 1866 Red Cloud led a massacre of 80 troops from Fort Kearny; this led to the abandonment of the fort by the whites in 1868. The fort was immediately burned to the ground by Red Cloud's triumphant warriors. More battles were fought in the vicinity of Fort Kearny than around any other fort on the western frontier.

Between Kearny and Laramie, travelers then and now pass several natural landmarks. Many pioneers scratched their names into the face of Chimney Rock, which rises 500 feet above the plains. Other interesting landmarks are Independence Rock and Scotts Bluff. Both loom from the surrounding prairies and serve as guides to those who wonder if this is indeed the correct route.

Fort Laramie, Wyoming's first permanent post, was established around 1834 by Jacques Laramie, a trapper for the American Fur Company. Here, all trails joined until they crossed South Pass. Fort Sanders, a short distance south, later provided protection for the Overland Stage Line and for the Union Pacific. The railroad brought the bulk of Laramie's citizenry, including a sizable population of lawless drifters who finally left town at the prompting of self-appointed vigilantes.

The city of Laramie was settled in 1868 as a tent and shanty town for workers building the Union Pacific Railroad. The railroad and ranching brought prosperity to the area. It now serves as the commercial, industrial, and transportation center for the surrounding sheep- and cattle-raising region. In 1851 the Fort Laramie Treaty established boundaries for the Plains tribes and guaranteed the safety of whites traveling the Oregon Trail.

Chief Red Cloud

Mahpiua Luta, or Red Cloud, a principal chief of the Oglala Sioux, lived near the banks of the Platte River in Nebraska in 1822. For years he was able to keep the United States government from opening up the West. However, a treaty in 1851 gave the whites the right to pass through Indian Territory. They proceeded to disregard the treaty by building forts and attempting to open roads.

Around 1860 when Red Cloud and his band were living near Fort Laramie, they attacked white immigrants who came onto Indian territory along the North Platte River. Later he effectively discouraged white travel on the Bozeman Trail. Red Cloud led the 1866 massacre of 80 troops from Fort Kearny, which had been built to protect the trail. At a council at Fort Laramie, Red Cloud repeated his refusal to endanger the hunting grounds of his people, and, angered by the lack of good faith of the whites, defiantly addressed his people in this manner:

> *Hear Ye, Dakotas. When the Great Father at Washington sent us his chief soldier (Major General William Harney) to ask for a path through our hunting grounds, a way for his iron horse and road to the mountains and the western sea, we were told that they wished merely to pass through our country, not to tarry among us but to seek gold in the far west. Our old chiefs thought to show their friendship and good will, when they allowed this dangerous snake in our midst. Yet before the ashes of the council fire are cold, the Great Father is building his forts among us. You have heard the sound of the white soldier's axe on Little Piney. His presence here is an insult and a threat. It is an insult to the spirits of our ancestors. Are we then to give up their sacred graves to be plowed for corn? Dakotas, I AM FOR WAR.*

A peace treaty which Red Cloud signed in 1868 seems to have been a turning point for the war chief. After visiting Washington, D.C., he recognized both the numbers and power of white people, so he agreed to settle down as a reservation chief. Sitting Bull and Crazy Horse both blamed him for allowing corrupt and unhealthy conditions on Sioux reservations. He quietly lived out the remainder of his life on the Pine Ridge Reservation in South Dakota. But his spirit lived on when, in 1973, members of the American Indian Movement seized the village of Wounded Knee to draw attention to Sioux grievances.

Make a poster divided like the sketch below. Tell how different Indian leaders felt about their land and culture and the changes that the white man brought.

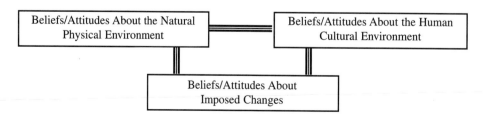

A Visit to Scotts Bluff

Scotts Bluff rises straight out of the flat farmlands of southwestern Nebraska to dominate the valley of the North Platte River. It is a towering rock formation that excites the imagination today just as it did for travelers on the Oregon Trail in the 1850s. For the buffalo-hunting Sioux it was the-hill-that-is-hard-to-go-around. For travelers on the Oregon Trail, it was a welcome landmark—a sign that wood and water would be close by.

Those leading the wagon trains knew that nearby Mitchell Pass would lead them behind the bluff and allow them to skirt the river badlands that were much too rough for wagons to cross. Wagons moved single file through the narrow gap, leaving ruts worn so deep that even today they can be seen. A short hike takes the visitor for a walk along the pioneer road where piñon trees and currant bushes dot the slopes.

Scotts Bluff entices all who see it. One early traveler wrote in his journal, "It has the appearance of castles and forts . . ." Another thought it "almost approaching the sublime." Today, Scotts Bluff is a national monument, maintained so that all Americans can walk through Mitchell Pass just as did the Prairie schooners, the Overland Stage, the Pony Express riders, and the first transcontinental telegraph. Of course, today's visitors have the advantage of asking for information from the rangers at the monument headquarters.

Imagine how it would be to visit Scotts Bluff. Write your impressions below.

A COVERED WAGON JOURNAL

A JOURNAL FROM TODAY

Once the travelers left Laramie, they left behind the clover fields of the Great Plains. It was time to cross the Rocky Mountains. They passed from the brown world of the desert to the green world of the mountains. The first travelers were the fur traders, then came the settlers' caravans, and finally the railroad builders.

South Pass was a natural wagon road between the headwaters of the North Platte and the headwaters of the South Snake. West of South Pass, the trail led to Fort Hall, where Nathaniel Wyeth beat the fur traders by building a fort to catch the trade of the Snake River Indians. He was forced to sell Fort Hall to his rivals, the Hudson's Bay Company.

The site of Fort Hall became the present-day city of Pocatello, named for a Bannock Indian chief. Lying on the Portneuf River near its junction with the Snake, the city was settled in the 1880s as a railroad center. Today, it is a processing center for farming and livestock. The area is known to many tourists because of the nearby ski area at Sun Valley. The name Fort Hall was retained for a reservation of about 3,000 Shoshone and Bannock Indians.

Another Hudson's Bay Company post at Fort Boise continued to serve the settlers traveling to the West over the Oregon and California Trails. It lies a few hours farther down the Snake River and west of the Rocky Mountains at an altitude of 2,740 ft. The city of Boise was founded after the 1862 gold rush in the Boise Basin. Later development was aided by lumbering and agricultural activities, especially after the start of the Boise Irrigation Project in 1902. Today, Boise is a wholesale trade and food-processing center for a large region in southwestern Idaho and eastern Oregon.

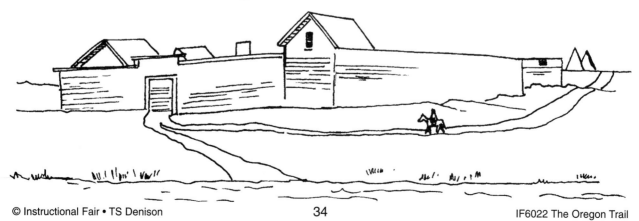

Making a Travel Brochure

The Oregon Trail crossed what are now the states of Missouri, Kansas, Nebraska, Wyoming, Idaho, and Oregon. From information you can get from various sources, including calling 800 numbers and using AAA books, create a brochure urging people to make a modern-day trip along the Old Oregon Trail. Tell them about both natural and man-made sights. Compare how they will travel, including meals and accommodations, with the manner in which the pioneers traveled in the mid-1800s.

Fold a piece of plain white paper in thirds, as shown.

Add pictures and sketches and writing.

Make people want to take the trip.

Fold an 8½" x 11" sheet of paper into thirds. On the front, include your title and an illustration. On the back, put your name as designer. On the inside, add information about various places on the trail.

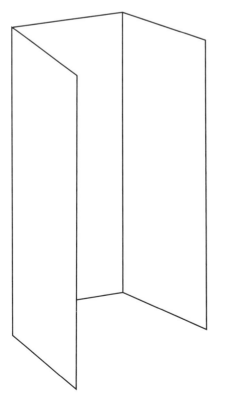

To get people to go on your trip, there are certain kinds of information you will need to provide. People will want to know about the cities they will visit and what they will be able to see.

For the sights you choose for your folder, be certain you have answered these questions:
    Where is it?
    What is it near?
    Why is it famous?

For the cities in your brochure, be certain you have answered questions like:
    How large is it?
    What is its relation to the trail?
    Are there any sights to see?
    How did it get its name?

Walla Walla was the pausing place in the march to the Columbia for almost a hundred years. The name means "place of many waters" in the Cayuse Indian language. The fur-trading post Fort Walla Walla was established in 1818. A military fort by the same name was established in 1856. A settlement, originally called Steptoeville, grew up around the military fort. Today, lumber yards, fruit and vegetable canneries, and grain processing are the basis of the economy.

Close to Walla Walla was the Indian mission established in 1836 by Marcus Whitman. Because of the Whitman massacre at Waiilatpu in 1847 and the Indian Wars that followed, settlement in the Columbia Basin was delayed for a number of years.

During the 1840s and 1850s, the Oregon Trail carried thousands of American pioneers to Fort Vancouver and the rich farmland of the Willamette Valley. Fort Vancouver is not to be confused with the city of Vancouver. This fort was built near where the Columbia River turns northward after it is joined by the Willamette.

The Willamette River flows northward to join the Columbia River near Portland. Today, it is widely used for irrigation and hydroelectricity and is navigable by small vessels.

Portland straddles the Willamette River just above its confluence with the Columbia. Named for Portland, Maine, the city was laid out in 1845. By 1860 it had become the largest city in the Pacific Northwest. The world's first long-distance electric transmission line, 14 miles long, brought power to the city in 1889.

Although Portland has some important manufacturing establishments, notably those turning out wood products and processed foods, its economy is primarily commercial. Today, this port is used by both barges carrying grain and ores downstream through the Columbia Gorge and oceangoing vessels, which can navigate the Columbia as far upstream as Portland.

The Route That Was Followed

The Oregon Trail was a long, rugged pathway carved by the footsteps, wagon wheels, and animals of people moving westward. The trail ran from Independence, Missouri, to the Oregon Country of the Pacific Northwest—about 2,000 miles. It wound through prairies, deserts, and mountains. During the mid 1800s, thousands upon thousands of pioneers journeyed west on this bumpy dirt track.

From Independence, the trail ran north and west to Fort Kearny in Nebraska. Next, it followed the wide, shallow Platte River west to Fort Laramie in Wyoming. From there, the trail continued along the North Platte River and its Sweetwater branch into the Rocky Mountains. At Fort Bridger, Wyoming, the trail turned north along the Snake River to Fort Hall and on to Fort Boise in Idaho. The final leg of the trail crossed the Blue Mountains, passed Fort Walla Walla in Washington, and then followed the Columbia River to the Willamette Valley.

TODAY'S ROUTE ALONG THE OREGON TRAIL

From:	To:	Route to Take:	Mileage:	Driving Time:
Kansas City, MO	Council Bluffs, IA			
Council Bluffs, IA	Kearny, NE			
Kearny, NE	Laramie, WY			
Laramie, WY	Boise, ID			
Boise, ID	Walla Walla, WA			
Walla Walla, WA	Portland, OR			

Weather and Climate

Using an almanac, atlas, or encyclopedia, find information about some cities along the Oregon Trail. Record your data in the chart below. Remember these are numbers that have been averaged over many years. So this is information about the climate rather than about weather.

DATA CHART ON CITIES OF THE OREGON TRAIL

Places along the Oregon Trail	Location	Average Summer Temp.	Average Winter Temp.	Altitude	Yearly Rainfall
Independence, MO					
Topeka, KS					
Kearny, NE					
Scotts Bluff, NE					
Laramie, WY					
Boise, ID					
Walla Walla, WA					
Portland, OR					

COMPARING INFORMATION

Rank Order by Height Above Sea Level
1. _____
2. _____
3. _____
4. _____
5. _____
6. _____
7. _____
8. _____

Rank Order by Amount of Rainfall
1. _____
2. _____
3. _____
4. _____
5. _____
6. _____
7. _____
8. _____

Rank Order by Winter Temperature
1. _____
2. _____
3. _____
4. _____
5. _____
6. _____
7. _____
8. _____

The Missouri River

The Missouri River begins at the junction of the Jefferson, Madison, and Gallatin Rivers in southwestern Montana. It flows well over 2,000 miles to join the Mississippi near St. Louis, Missouri.

The upper Missouri River flows eastward across the high plains of Montana and joins the Yellowstone River near the North Dakota border. It then flows southward across the high plains of North and South Dakota. At this point, it marks the boundary between the humid grain-farming area to the east and the more arid cattle-grazing lands to the west.

Many rivers flow into the Missouri River. Continuing southeastward, it meets the Platte River near Omaha and Council Bluffs and flows on to Kansas City, where the Kansas River enters from the west. The river's course turns eastward across Missouri to Saint Louis, where it joins the Mississippi. Together with all of its tributaries, the Missouri drains about 530,000 square miles of land. This area is called the Missouri River basin.

Early inhabitants of the Missouri valley included the Cheyenne, Crow, Mandan, Pawnee, and Sioux Indians. In 1673 the French explorers Jacques Marquette and Louis Jolliet were the first white people to see the Missouri. Traders and settlers soon used the river as a canoe pathway into the Missouri River basin. Manufactured goods were sent in by canoe or shallow-bottomed boat. Furs, hides, and grains were shipped out. Fur trading was the area's primary activity until steamboat traffic and agricultural settlement became important by the 1840s.

During the 1800s steamboats carried goods up and down the river. Many pioneers going west traveled by steamer on the Missouri. After the completion of the first bridge across the Missouri River in 1869, Kansas City became a transportation hub. Railroads were built across the basin in the late 1800s after which there was less traffic on the river.

The Platte River System

The Platte River is a 310-mile tributary of the Missouri River. The 680-mile North Platte begins in the Rocky Mountains of north central Colorado and flows north into Wyoming before entering Nebraska. The 442-mile South Platte starts in central Colorado. The branches join at the city of North Platte in central Nebraska. The Platte River then flows east to join the Missouri River just south of Omaha. The river is extremely shallow except during the spring, which makes it unsuitable for boat traffic. Its principal economic value is as a source of irrigation water. The Platte system drains an area of about 90,000 square miles.

Explored as early as 1739 by the French and in 1820 by Stephen H. Long, the river valley was one of the main routes for pioneers using the Oregon and Mormon Trails. The Union Pacific Railroad, the first rail link between the eastern and western United States, ran through the valley as well.

The main Oregon Trail ran west along the Platte and North Platte Rivers to Fort Laramie. The area was inhabited by the northern Cheyenne. The Cheyenne were constantly at war with the Kiowa, Apache, and Comanche until 1840, when an alliance was formed.

The Snake River

An important route to the Pacific Northwest, the Snake River was discovered by the Lewis and Clark Expedition in 1805 and was used by pioneers traveling the Oregon Trail.

The Snake River, in the northwestern United States, is the largest tributary of the Columbia River. It begins in the Rocky Mountains of western Wyoming, flows into eastern Idaho, and twists and meanders across the Columbia Plateau, a region of high, rolling plains. Then it flows north through Hell's Canyon, becoming part of the border between Idaho and Oregon. With its tributaries—the Wind, Bruneau, Salmon, Powder, Clearwater, and Palouse Rivers—the Snake drains an area of 109,000 square miles. Most of the people in Idaho live on or near farmlands irrigated by the Snake River.

The Snake then flows generally west and southwest to join the Columbia at Burbank, Washington. Several areas of rapids and waterfalls occur along the river, which has been dammed in many places for power and irrigation. Wildlife is still abundant along the river, especially in several national parks and recreational areas.

Along this part of the river is Hell's Canyon, the deepest gorge in North America. In some places, the gorge is 8,000 feet deep—more than a mile and a half from rim to bottom. Hell's Canyon is more than 100 miles long.

The Columbia River

From the high meadows of western Canada, the Columbia River flows through great, forested mountains and down desert canyons. After it has been joined by the Snake River, it rolls with increased force through fertile flat lands, past snow-covered volcanoes, and through a final mountain range to complete a 1,200-mile journey to the sea. This grand gateway to the West was traversed by courageous settlers as they forged their way over the Oregon Trail to the fertile Willamette Valley. Commercial fishing, especially for salmon, has been important since the 1860s, although the catch has been greatly curtailed by over-fishing and habitat destruction.

The Columbia River was the main Indian pathway from the Rocky Mountains to the sea, and it forms an important section of the Old Oregon Trail. Lewis and Clark, who led the first white men to travel the river to the Pacific, were followed by a host of fur traders and mountain men. When settlers began the long and arduous trip to the valleys of Oregon, they found the river too rough for floating their wagons. Therefore, roads had to be carved along the steep riverbanks.

The most spectacular part of this river is the 60-mile stretch through a narrow canyon known as the Columbia River Gorge. This stretch includes beautiful creeks, spectacular falls, and little creeks that drop into the great river in steep falls or rushing white water rapids that plunge into quiet pools.

The Columbia was discovered by a Boston trader, Robert Gray, in 1792 and named for his ship. It was explored by Lewis and Clark in 1805, and the river gorge through the Cascade Range became an early transportation route. By the 1850s, steamboats were operating in spite of the frequent rapids. Improvements, including canals, came later.

The Columbia River is a major waterway of the northwestern United States and southwestern Canada. Fed by rain and snow from the mountains of British Columbia, Canada, it flows 1,210 miles, first northwestward and then south. The headwaters include several large glacial lakes. Important tributaries are the Kootenay, Snake, and Willamette Rivers.

Student Activities

THINKING ABOUT THE READING

What does it mean for a river to twist and meander? Does that give you a clue about how the Snake River got its name? Explain:

_____

_____

_____

_____

_____

Salmon on the Columbia River

After the building of huge dams such as the Bonneville, the salmon could no longer reach their spawning beds. Fish ladders were built to help them reach the fresh water where they could lay their eggs and complete their life cycle. The fish ladders are a series of terraced pools that lead from river level to the top of the dam. Salmon as big as 50 pounds can hurl themselves from pool to pool against the tumbling water. After spawning, exhausted and starving, they will die. But their tiny offspring will repeat the remarkable cycle of salmon life. First, they grow in fresh water to fingerling size; then they migrate down the river to the Pacific, where they spread out as far as the Bering Sea and the Aleutian Islands. Years later, grown to full size, they return, journeying unerringly back up the Columbia and other Western rivers. They will reach the waters of the very creek or river inlet where they were born—and where they in turn will spawn, starting the life cycle once again.

All salmon are not alike. Different kinds include:

- The *silver*, which is the most adaptable salmon. This eight-pound silver thrives in most of Oregon's coastal streams, spawning both near salt water and in fresh headwaters.

- The ten-pound *chum* prefers spawning close to salt water, in a lagoon or tide pool fed by a freshwater stream. The young go to sea almost at once.

- The fierce-looking *sockeye* grows up to 12 pounds. It spawns only in streams headed by lakes. The young stay there for a year before migrating out to the ocean.

- The *Chinook* varies from 10 to 45 pounds. The Chinook or king is the largest of this group. It is the most wide-ranging and produces the most offspring. One female will average 6,000 eggs.

Make a poster about saving the salmon. Remember to:

    Keep the title big

    Make it colorful

    Include ways to help prevent problems.

To add a 3-D display to the bottom of your poster, make two open pyramids as shown below. Remember to illustrate before gluing.

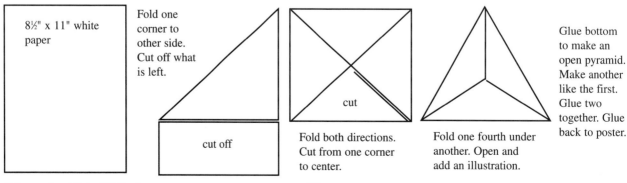

8½" x 11" white paper

Fold one corner to other side. Cut off what is left.

cut off

Fold both directions. Cut from one corner to center.

cut

Fold one fourth under another. Open and add an illustration.

Glue bottom to make an open pyramid. Make another like the first. Glue two together. Glue back to poster.

Answer Key

Investigating the Oregon Country   **Page 2**
1. furs, China
2. sail into the Columbia River
3. Astoria, John Jacob Astor
4. Nathaniel Wyeth, schoolteacher
5. Indians, American settlers
6. Louisiana Purchase

Lewis and Clark Activities   **Page 4**
1. Thomas Jefferson
2. Lewis and Clark
3. $2500
4. Sacajawea; Answers will vary.
5. It is usually easier to travel by water. Rivers are a path from mountain to sea. Exploring them means the pathway's territory has been explored.

Trappers and Traders   **Page 6**
1. mountain men
2. South Pass
3. Manuel Lisa
4. Sierra Nevada
5. beaver hats
6. leading settlers

Explorer Riddles   **Page 7**
William Clark
Meriwether Lewis
James Beckwourth
Jedediah Smith
Manuel Lisa
Thomas Fitzpatrick

Thinking About the Missionaries   **Page 9**
1. Pierre Jean De Smet
2. Iowa, Montana, Oregon
3. Marcus Whitman

4. near present-day Walla Walla, Washington
5. measles
6. She was killed by Cayuse Indians.
Discussion answers will vary.

Oregon Trail People History Cards   **Pages 10-12**
Sacajawea—a, c
Lewis—c, b
Clark—c, a
Lisa—b, a
Whitman—b, c
De Smet—b, c
Smith—c, a
Beckwourth—b, a

Talking Stick Discussions   **Page 15**
Answers will vary.

Native-American History Cards   **Page 16**
Washakie—a, b
Sitting bull—c, a
Red Cloud—a, c

On to Oregon   **Page 18**
1. Oregon Country
2. Independence
3. gold
4. six
5. 1843

11 miles

Great Trails of the West   **Page 19**

Living the Life of the Trail   **Page 21**
1. handcart
2. Conestoga
3. protect from the Indians, keep cattle from wandering off
4. water, rivers
5. captain, guides

Hardships examples:
flooded rivers had to be crossed
illness from cholera and other diseases
sickness from the heat or the altitude
broken wagon axles
scared by coyote howls
fresh meat and wood hard to find
unsafe water holes

Fighting the Fight   Page 23
1. Jim Bridger
2. Red Cloud
3. Fetterman, firewood
4. guns, bullets
5. Red Cloud, 1,137

Thinking It Over: possible answers
1. signaling, ambush
2. formed a circle fort, prepared with extra rifles, on a hill without dry grass

Cultural Differences   Pages 24 & 25
Answers will vary.

Railroads and the West   Page 27
1. Grenville Dodge
2. fighting, Civil War
3. Washington, Percy Brown's
4. government commissioner, military
5. North Platte, snow

Thinking It Over: possible answers
1. built railroads, inspired others, recognized need for speed
2. He faced the dangers he asked others to face.
3. He inspired them and showed them how not to be afraid.
4. He was willing to do himself what he asked of others.

A Western Fort   Page 29
1. supplies, wagons
2. South Pass, Green
3. They provided fire-resistance and insulation.
4. Walla Walla, Whitmans
5. Father De Smet, St. Louis

Comparing What People Remember

Memories	Mountain Men	Sioux Warrior	Pioneer
How I traveled:	I walked.	I rode horseback.	I walked beside the wagon or rode in it.
Problems I faced:	I was alone. The beaver got trapped out.	The white man was killing buffalo, taking land, bringing disease.	Travel was hard. Wagons broke down. People got sick.
What I saw:	I saw beautiful mountains and streams and lots of animals.	I saw many strangers coming across the plains.	I saw prairies, mountains, and fertile land for the taking.
How I used the land:	I lived off the animals but I killed them for skins more than for food.	I was one with the land. It gave me what I needed.	I wanted to farm the land and raise crops.
People I knew:	I met other trappers. I was separated from family.	I had my family and the other members of the tribe.	I had my family. I met all the people in my wagon train.
Things I did for fun:	We all got together for a rendezvous and had a big party.	My tribe had ceremonies where we told stories of bravery.	The people on the train got together to sing and talk around the campfire.

The Route That Was Followed   Page 37

From:	To:	Route to Take:	Mileage:	Driving Time:
Kansas City, MO	Council Bluffs, IA	Interstate 29	190 mi.	4 hours
Council Bluffs, IA	Kearny, NE	Interstate 80	175 mi.	3.5 hours
Kearny, NE	Laramie, WY	Interstate 80	360 mi.	7 hours
Laramie, WY	Boise, ID	Interstate 80 and Interstate 84	660 mi.	13 hours
Boise, ID	Walla Walla, WA	Interstate 84 and Route 395	235 mi.	3.5 hours
Walla Walla, WA	Portland, OR	Route 730 and Interstate 84	200 mi.	4 hours

Weather and Climate   Page 38
Height Above Sea Level:
1. Portland
2. Independence
3. Topeka
4. Walla Walla
5. Kearny
6. Boise
7. Scotts Bluff
8. Laramie

Amount of Rainfall:
1. Boise
2. Laramie
3. Walla Walla
4. Scotts Bluff
5. Kearny
6. Independence
7. Topeka
8. Portland

Winter Temperature:
1. Boise
2. Laramie
3. Walla Walla
4. Scotts Bluff
5. Independence
6. Kearny
7. Topeka
8. Portland

Places along the Oregon Trail	Location	Average Summer Temp.	Average Winter Temp.	Altitude	Yearly Rainfall
Independence, MO	38°N 94°W	80°	28°	800'	30"
Topeka, KS	39°N 95°W	75°	30°	877'	34"
Kearny, NE	41°N 99°W	77°	20°	2600'	30"
Scotts Bluff, NE	42°N 104°W	76°	21°	2800'	25"
Laramie, WY	41°N 106°W	68°	26°	6700'	13"
Boise, ID	43°N 116°W	70°	35°	2700'	12"
Walla Walla, WA	46°N 118°W	70°	25°	1700'	16"
Portland, OR	45°N 122°W	64°	39°	210'	37"

Rivers of the Trail   Page 41
Student Activities:
Twist means "to turn from side to side" or "to wind as a path." *Meander* means "to wind or wander." The Snake got its name because it winds or wanders through the countryside, much as a snake winds to move.